Aunts

by Lola M. Schaefer

Consulting Editor: Gail Saunders-Smith, Ph.D.

Consultant: Phyllis Edelbrock, First-Grade Teacher,
University Place School District, Washington

Pebble Books

an imprint of Capstone Press
Mankato, Minnesota

1

Pebble Books are published by Capstone Press
818 North Willow Street, Mankato, Minnesota 56001
http://www.capstone-press.com

Library of Congress Cataloging-in-Publication Data
Schaefer, Lola M., 1950–
       Aunts/by Lola M. Schaefer.
       p. cm.—(Families)
       Includes bibliographical references and index.
       Summary: Simple text and photographs depict aunts, where they live, and what
they do.
       ISBN 0-7368-0252-5
       1. Aunts—Juvenile literature. 2. Nieces—Juvenile literature. 3. Nephews—
Juvenile literature. [1. Aunts.] I. Title. II. Series: Schaefer, Lola M., 1950–   Families.
HQ759.94.S33   1999
306.87—dc21   98-46120
                                                                                            CIP
                                                                                            AC

Note to Parents and Teachers

The Families series supports national social studies standards for units related to identifying family members and their roles in the family. This book describes and illustrates aunts and activities they do with their nieces and nephews. The photographs support emergent readers in understanding the text. The repetition of words and phrases helps emergent readers learn new words. This book also introduces emergent readers to subject-specific vocabulary words, which are defined in the Words to Know section. Emergent readers may need assistance to read some words and to use the Table of Contents, Words to Know, Read More, Internet Sites, and Index/Word List sections of the book.

2

Table of Contents

sisters

mother

son

nephew

aunt

4

Aunts are sisters of
mothers or fathers.

aunt

Canada

United States

niece

Mexico

6

An aunt can live
far away.

This aunt sends letters.

This aunt calls on
the phone.

This aunt comes by airplane.

14

An aunt can live nearby.

This aunt comes to birthday parties.

This aunt comes to
hockey games.

Aunts come to play.

Words to Know

airplane—a machine with wings and engines that flies through the air; people ride in airplanes to travel long distances.

aunt—the sister of a person's mother or father; an aunt also can be the wife of a person's uncle.

father—a male parent

hockey—a game played on ice; skaters use sticks to try to hit a puck into the other team's net.

letter—a written note or message that is sent to someone

mother—a female parent

nearby—close, not far away

sister—a girl or woman who has the same parents as another person

Read More

Miller, Margaret. *Family Time.* A Super Chubby Board Book. New York: Little Simon, 1996.

Saunders-Smith, Gail. *Families.* People. Mankato, Minn.: Pebble Books, 1998.

Skutch, Robert. *Who's in a Family?* Berkeley, Calif.: Tricycle Press, 1995.

Internet Sites

Aunts and Uncles
http://www.firstct.com/fv/aunt.html

Family.com
http://family.go.com

Family First
http://hometown.aol.com/BMValen/index.html

Living Genealogy and Family Reunion Awards
http://www.firstct.com/fv/dori.html

Index/Word List

airplane, 13
away, 7
birthday, 17
calls, 11
come, 13, 17, 19, 21
far, 7
fathers, 5
games, 19
hockey, 19

letters, 9
live, 7, 15
mothers, 5
nearby, 15
parties, 17
phone, 11
play, 21
sends, 9
sisters, 5

Word Count: 49
Early-Intervention Level: 5

Editorial Credits
Mari C. Schuh, editor; Steve Weil/Tandem Design, cover designer;
    Linda Clavel, illustrator; Kimberly Danger, photo researcher

Photo Credits
David F. Clobes, 1
Diane G. Hillman, 6 (bottom)
Mark Turner, 4, 8 (left and right), 10 (top and bottom), 12, 14, 18
PhotoBank, Inc./Bill Lai, cover
Photri-Microstock/David Lissy, 16
R. S. Lyle Hillman, M.D., 6 (top)
Uniphoto, 20

Special thanks to Joy Allison, Lori Hollenback, and Penny McCarthy, first-grade
teachers at Evergreen Primary in University Place, Washington, for reviewing the
books in the Families series.